My Parrot Eats Baked Beans

kids talk about their pets

My Parrot Eats Baked Beans

kids talk about their pets

Written and Photographed by Barbara Garland Polikoff

Albert Whitman & Company · Niles, Illinois

Library of Congress Cataloging-in-Publication Data

Polikoff, Barbara Garland.
   My parrot eats baked beans.

   Summary: Eight young pet owners recount their
experiences with and feelings for their pets.
   1. Pets—Anecdotes—Juvenile literature. [1. Pets]
I. Title.
SF416.2.P65 1988   636.08′87   88-21
ISBN 0-8075-5349-2

Text and photographs © 1988 by Barbara Garland Polikoff
Design by Gordon Stromberg
Published in 1988 by Albert Whitman & Company, Niles, Illinois
Published simultaneously in Canada
by General Publishing, Limited, Toronto
10   9   8   7   6   5   4   3   2   1

For Alexander

Table of Contents

Giselle, Creamy, and Gaia

I have animal friends in two houses. In my own house, I have my guinea pigs—Pizza and Buffy and their three children, Pepperoni, Olive, and Whitey. In the house across the street, I have the Matlins' Siberian Husky, Gaia.

I spend a lot of time with my animals. They keep me company after school on days Mom has to work and my big sister, Erica, has sports and band practice.

I don't like walking into a quiet house with no one in it, so I always yell to my guinea pigs, "I'm home!" It's better to hear my own voice than no voice at all. I bring the guinea pigs up from the basement where they live, and we have something to eat together. I have juice and cookies or a peanut-butter-and-banana sandwich, and they have lettuce and carrots. I like hearing them munch their food.

Sometimes my guinea pigs watch me work on the life history charts that Erica and I are making for each of them. We write down everything important about their lives: when they were born, if they're married, what they eat, if they have any allergies, and what their

jobs are. We decided Buffy must be in the real estate business because he always runs from room to room, checking up on things.

In nice weather, I take the guinea pigs outside so they can play on the grass. Buffy is the one I have to watch. Pizza and her babies are happy to stay near me and nibble the clover and feel the sun, but Buffy runs off to check things out just like he does in the house. Once I really thought I had lost him. Was I glad when he scampered from under a big, leafy bush! When I stretch out, Pizza scrambles all over my chest and stomach and down my legs. Her little feet tickle.

Playing with Gaia is very different. She loves to jump on me, and her paws don't tickle! If I roll on the grass with her, she licks my face and tries to chew on my ears. Once I played a trick on her—I came over to play with earmuffs on. She tried chewing them, too. She stopped when she got a mouthful of blue fuzz.

Gaia loves to nap under the oak tree in the Matlins' yard. Because she doesn't like warm weather, she sleeps a lot in the summer. Then I can put my head on her, and we rest together. She's the softest pillow in the world! I fell asleep once resting on her, and my mom got worried. She didn't know where I was. That was the time my best friend, Susan, left me out of a picnic she had with some other kids, and I was feeling awful. Gaia is so jumpy and peppy most of the time. But she can be very peaceful, too. Sometimes, when I'm crabby, she makes me feel more peaceful.

Now I'm going to tell you a terrible thing that happened to Creamy, Pizza's first baby. It was the day school ended, and I had my guinea pigs out on the grass. The sun was pretty bright, so I put out a pillow that they could crawl under for shade. The babies loved it under there. Well, I was happy school was over, and I was just kind of daydreaming. I didn't notice Gaia and Mrs. Matlin until it was too late. Gaia ran to see me, but then she smelled the guinea pigs. Before I could do anything, she pushed her head under the pillow and grabbed Creamy. I was so scared I screamed. Mrs. Matlin yelled and yanked the leash real hard. Gaia dropped Creamy on the ground.

I ran and picked him up, trying to be very careful. When I brought him into the house, I saw that he had two teeth marks on his neck. But they weren't bleeding, so I figured he was all right. I fixed up a small basket with a very soft blanket and put him in it to rest.

When Erica came home, I told her what had happened. She looked at Creamy to see how he was doing. Then she lifted him out of the basket.

"Giselle," she said. "Creamy's dead."

I couldn't believe it. I started to cry and couldn't stop until my mom came home. She and Erica and I fixed a tiny grave out in the backyard where our bunny, Popcorn, is buried. I found a flat stone. On it I

wrote, "Creamy, whose life was too short. May 16 – June 24, 1987."
I put the stone at the head of the grave, and Erica put a little vase of
pansies next to it. She tried to make me feel better, but nothing that
she said helped.

I didn't go to play with Gaia after that. I wouldn't even look at her.

One day Mrs. Matlin came to talk to me while I was outside waiting
for my mom.

"You haven't visited Gaia for so long," she said. "Are you still angry
with her?"

I told her I was even though I knew it would make her feel bad.
She said she knew how I felt. Once she had been angry at Gaia for
a whole day when Gaia caught a squirrel and it died. She didn't take
her for a walk or give her any treats.

When I asked her what made her stop being angry at Gaia, she
told me how she began thinking that Gaia was just doing what animals
do. If she were in the wilderness, she would have to kill other animals
for food or she'd die. Just because she lived in a yard and was given
food on a plate didn't mean she would stop hunting animals.

"But Creamy was so little," I told her. "He was my favorite."

13

FILE | NAME: PEPPERONI   SEX: MALE

MOTHER: PIZZA   FATHER: BUFFY

JOB:

BORN: OCTOBER 1st 1985 | MODEL

PICTURE: | M. STATUS: SINGLE

LENGTH: 11.5 INCHES

WIDTH: 11.7 INCHES

RELATIVES: CREAM PUFF, PINKLET

REGISTRATION: AUGUST 31st, 1986

LAST DOCTOR APPT: JUNE 15th

Sicknesses		FOODS:			
HAY FEVER	✓	BARLEY		GRASS ✗	ALFALFA ✗
COM. COLD	✓	CARROTS	✓	FLOWERS	PELLETS ✗
DROWSINESS	✓	LETTUCE	✓	WHEAT	SALT ✗
		S PROUTS		APPLE ✓	WATER ✓
DIRRHEA	✓			BANANA	OATS ✗
					SUGAR ✗

RECORDS: EVERY 1/2 YEAR

ADDRESS: CREAMY CONDOS | IQ: 10+

PAW PRINTS (LFT) (RFT.) | FUR SAMPLE

ALLERGIES:
TOMATOES   DOGS
PEANUTS   BEES

COLOR:
BUFF AND WHITE

Mrs. Matlin talked about Pizza's babies and how they nuzzle right up to Pizza and start nursing almost as soon as they're born. She asked me if anybody taught the babies to do that. Of course, I said no. Then she said it was the same for Gaia. She was doing what came naturally to her when she smelled the babies under the pillow and grabbed Creamy.

14

I thought about what Mrs. Matlin said when I was lying in bed that night. I loved watching the baby guinea pigs falling all over each other to get Pizza's milk. And then I thought about how I used to be scared of Gaia when I was little because I thought she was a wolf. Mrs. Matlin told me that Gaia came from the same family wolves did. If she were still in the woods, I couldn't be mad at her for killing animals for food. I guessed it was the wolf in her that made her grab Creamy.

I got up real early the next day and went over to the Matlins' yard. Gaia was sleeping under the oak tree. I sat down next to her and scratched her ears.

"I'm not mad at you anymore," I told her.

She licked my nose.

When I said, "Let's go for a walk," she jumped up and ran to the gate. I got the leash from Mrs. Matlin, and we walked to the park. Every time Gaia saw a squirrel, her ears went up and her tail went down. One squirrel ran so close to her that I yelled, "Hey, Dummy! Get away!"

It felt good being friends with Gaia again.

Now I want to tell you some good news. Pizza just had three babies. I named the white one Creamy, Junior.

A Tip from Giselle: *If you take your guinea pigs outside, you have to watch them every minute!*

Brian and Uncle Feather

My parrot, Uncle Feather, knows what he likes. If I give him a spoonful of cold baked beans to eat, he drops the spoon on the floor and the baked beans go splattering. If I put the beans in the microwave for a minute and give them back, he eats them right away and wants more. Me, I'll eat baked beans hot or cold.

Everyone is surprised to see Uncle Feather holding a spoon and eating. But parrots are good at using their claws. A wild parrot is always flying from tree to tree and using his claws to perch on different-size branches. So it's easy for a parrot to hold something as thin as a spoon handle or as fat as a big branch. Changing perches gives a parrot's claws good exercise, too. That's why you have to give a pet parrot different-size perches in his cage. Once friends took care of Uncle Feather for us when we went on vacation. They switched him to a nice big cage, but it had only one skinny perch. Poor Uncle Feather got blisters on his claws. Little pink ones.

My dad made Uncle Feather a great perch that's branched like a tree. Uncle Feather really likes it. He'll even sleep on it, standing on one leg and burying his head in his back feathers. One little kid saw Uncle Feather sleeping like that and got scared that his head had fallen off!

Living with Uncle Feather for two and a half years—that's how old he is—has helped me know his ways. Of everyone in the family, I've paid the most attention to him, and so he's my bird more than my brother Stephen's or Mom's or Dad's. Parrots pick the person that spends a lot of time with them to be their favorite. I kind of like that. It's fun to have Uncle Feather like me the best.

Just after we got Uncle Feather, we went to Disneyland and I asked the bird expert on Paradise Island how to train a parrot. He told me that when you put your finger out for him to perch on, don't pull it back if he tries to bite it. Push your finger right into his beak instead! If you pull away from him, he thinks, "Hey, I'm the boss here," and that's no good. But if he sees you're not afraid of him, he'll stop biting you, and you'll be able to train him. So that's what I did. Now Uncle Feather's so used to me that he doesn't nip me. Every once in a while, when we're playing, he'll give me a kiss.

The great thing about having a parrot for a pet is that you don't have to see them get old and die when they're fourteen or fifteen, like a dog or cat. They can live to be eighty years old! It's kind of great but weird, too. My mom said that when I'm old enough to get married, I'd better find a girl who likes Uncle Feather because where I go, Uncle Feather goes. If I have children, they'll be able to play with Uncle Feather. When I think of that, it makes me feel a little funny.

I don't know if Uncle Feather can keep learning new words for eighty years. He's learned so many already: "Bye, bye, see you later," "Hi, Baby," "Pretty bird," "What's your name?" and "I love you." He knows the whole family's names. He calls Dad "Bill," but he doesn't use Mom's name, Sally Jo. She's just "Mom." That's because he hears

Stephen and me calling "Mom!" a hundred times a day. In a way, he chose "Uncle Feather" for himself. We got the name from a book we liked. We meant to call him that for a little while until we thought of a name that fit him. But he learned to say "Uncle Feather" so fast we figured he liked that name. He talks so well that when Mom calls, "Brian," he answers, "What?" She thinks it's me! He just learned to imitate the smoke alarm. That's not great. When we hear this beeping, we have to check where it's coming from—the alarm or Uncle Feather!

The first spring we had Uncle Feather, something real scary happened. Since Uncle Feather likes to be out on sunny days, we put him in the yard on his perch. His wing feathers are clipped so he can't fly.

If you keep a parrot in your house, you have to do that. Well, just as I put him outside, Stephen started our lawn mower. The noise frightened Uncle Feather so much he took off and flew across the street into a big maple tree. The vet hadn't clipped his feathers short enough! I ran yelling, "Uncle Feather! Uncle Feather!" I was scared he would fly off somewhere and not be able to come back because he wouldn't recognize our house from the rooftop.

I grabbed a long stick I use to get frisbees and kites out of trees and started climbing up the maple, talking to Uncle Feather the whole time. I could see him on a branch way up at the top. My mom kept calling, "Brian, don't go so high!" But I had to go high enough to be able to reach the stick out to Uncle Feather so he would perch on it.

Lots of people from the neighborhood were down on the sidewalk watching. I saw them but I didn't see them, you know what I mean? All I could think of was Uncle Feather and how I had to get him on that stick. Mom said I kept talking and talking to Uncle Feather, never stopping for a whole half-hour. And then he stepped off the branch onto the stick! I couldn't get excited and jerk the stick or he'd get scared. So I climbed down carefully, praying all the time that Uncle Feather wouldn't fly off.

He didn't. He stayed with me the whole time. When I got down to the sidewalk, the people were smart enough not to yell or clap and scare Uncle Feather. I walked holding my breath until he was safely in the house. I was so happy I hugged him. (Yes, you can hug a bird!) I kept telling him what a good parrot he was, and I gave him all the warm baked beans he could eat. After that, before we took him outside, we were extra careful to make sure his wing feathers were clipped short enough.

Everyone says it's pretty amazing that I climbed up that tree and kept talking to Uncle Feather for a whole half-hour. And it was pretty amazing that he came to me that way.

It makes me feel good to think that Uncle Feather can live with me the rest of my life, even if I live to be ninety. My dad said we'll be two old birds together.

A Tip from Brian: Be sure to give your parrot a lot of different-size perches to climb on so he can exercise his claws.

Maya and Autumn

Autumn used to be my friend Betsy's cat. But now she's mine. This is how it happened.

Betsy asked me if I would take care of Autumn while her family went on a vacation. I said OK without even asking my mom. Autumn was such a nice cat, and I figured Mom wouldn't tell me to say no to Betsy.

Autumn came to our house at a good time because my dad had moved out to live in Baltimore. He and my mom were getting a divorce. So it wasn't just Mom and me in the house. It was Mom, me, and Autumn.

Autumn made us laugh with the funny things she did. She found my old Barbie dolls on a shelf and took the blond wig off one of them and played with it like a ball. She got to know when I was feeling grumpy or lonesome for Daddy. She would go to the Barbie dolls and get the blond wig—never the brown or red one—and bring it to me as if she wanted to make me feel better. I liked the way she would curl up next to me when I was reading on the chair with my stuffed animals.

The day we had to give Autumn back to Betsy, I kept hoping something would happen so I could keep her. Betsy and her mom came in the afternoon, and I stayed in my room. I came out when Autumn was gone. The house seemed so different without her—kind of quiet. Even though she hardly ever made any noise.

Then Betsy's family moved to a bigger apartment, and the landlady didn't want any animals. Betsy was sure she'd change her mind. She asked me if I'd keep Autumn until she did. Autumn lived with us for one month. Then it was two months. Then it was three months. The landlady didn't change her mind, so I didn't have to pretend Autumn was my cat anymore. She really was. I felt sorry for Betsy. I told her she should come and play with Autumn anytime she wanted to.

I hoped Autumn liked living with me as much as with Betsy. I wasn't really sure.

This is the worst part of the story. I was going to visit my dad in Baltimore on spring vacation. I hugged Autumn a lot before I had to leave and told her I'd be back soon. But when I opened the door to walk out with my duffel, she ran out, too. I chased down the porch steps after her, but she disappeared into the neighbor's yard. And then I didn't see her anymore.

I wanted to stay so I could look for her. Autumn's a house cat, and I was afraid of what might happen to her outside. But Mom was in the car with the motor running. She got out and grabbed my duffel, telling me I'd better come that second or I'd miss the plane. She said that Autumn would probably be on the porch when she got back from the airport, but that didn't make me feel any better.

Autumn wasn't on the porch. I found that out when Dad and I called Mom the minute we got into his house in Baltimore. We called almost every day after that. Each time, my mom told me the same thing. Autumn hadn't come back.

I had all these bad ideas in my head about Autumn getting lost and not being able to find her way back home. Would someone find her and bring her to their house for keeps? What if another animal started a fight with her? I wished there was a button I could push to stop all those bad thoughts.

Even though I wanted to see my mom, I didn't want to go back home without Autumn being there. I had to, though, and when Mom picked me up at the airport, I tried to act happy so she wouldn't feel bad.

The minute I walked into our yard, I started looking for Autumn and calling her name. I didn't really think she was there, but I did it anyway. And Mom kept telling me to come into the house.

And then I heard a noise. I listened hard. "Mommy," I said. "I hear Autumn!"

"It's just the rustling of the leaves," she told me.

I heard the noise again. "It's Autumn. I know!"

Then Autumn jumped on the porch railing next to me so fast I didn't know where she came from! I grabbed her and hugged her and hugged her.

Then I walked into the house with Autumn, and Wow! People popped up from behind the furniture yelling, "Welcome home, Maya!" I saw my grandpop and two aunts and two of my friends and a neighbor. There were balloons all over, and lots of food on the table. I was so surprised!

"It's a welcome home party for Autumn, too," I said. "I went on a trip, and so did she."

Everybody yelled, "Welcome home, Autumn!"

I never found out where Autumn went. All I know is that she was gone two weeks and came back the minute I came home. Now I'm sure she's my cat for real.

A Tip from Maya: *If you have a house cat, be careful when you open an outside door!*

Todd and His Suffolk Sheep

I slept at the County Fair last night with a bunch of other 4-H kids. Hay makes a pretty good bed except your clothes get full of it. The fair lasts five days, and you get to be with kids from all over the county. They're here to show their cows, horses, chickens, pigs, and sheep. Even rabbits. You remember who won prizes last year and wonder who's going to win the big prizes this year. You do a lot of talking and joking and a lot of waiting around.

Today I'm showing my Suffolk sheep, so I woke up feeling a little nervous. My brother Kurt's been showing Suffolks at different fairs for eight years, and he still gets nervous. I guess that's the way it is. It's a good kind of nervous, though. Not like being nervous about finding out if you flunked a test or not.

I got my first Suffolk ewe—that's a female sheep—four years ago when I was eight. My two brothers had sheep, and I got to like them a lot. Right now we have twenty-two Suffolks on our farm. We raise some for wool and some for meat. Eight of the twenty-two are mine. There isn't too much I have to do to take care of my sheep except feed

them twice a day. In the winter, when it's dark and freezing out, I'd like to stay in bed a little longer instead of feeding them, but I never do.

I have a favorite ewe that I'm going to keep with me for her whole life. Her mother and father were pretty small, ordinary sheep, so I didn't expect their lamb to be anything special. Was I surprised when I saw her out in the barn for the first time! She was just a couple of days old, but I could tell she'd be a prize sheep. She was a good size, and did she grow fast! Right now, she's in Utah being mated with a prize ram.

This Utah sheepman picks up sheep at different places—we brought mine all the way to Des Moines, Iowa, about three hundred miles away. Then he takes them back to his ranch to mate with his ram. In a week, we'll have to drive six hundred miles again to pick up my ewe and bring her home. If she doesn't have a lamb in the spring, I get to send her back to Utah, but next time it's free.

This morning I'm showing three yearling ewes. Yearlings are one year old. I started getting them ready a while ago. We sheared them so their fleece would grow back just enough to look right for the fair. Kurt went to a sheep-shearing school at the University of Illinois, and he's really good at it. He can get the whole hide off in one piece—like taking off a big sweater. He's teaching me what he learned, and if I practice maybe I can get as good as he is.

Then, a day before the fair, we wash the sheep. They don't like that, and we have to strap them to a stand so they'll stay still. I guess I wouldn't like someone giving me a cold shower, either! To start out, we turn a hose on them. Their wool is so thick and full of lanolin that at first the water is just soaked up and you can't even tell it's there.

We have to spray almost fifteen gallons on a sheep before the wool is wet enough to work the shampoo in. And rubbing that shampoo into their thick wool takes a lot of energy. But the wool dries white and clean, and then when you trim it and use a currycomb to take the tangles out, the sheep really look neat. Afterwards, you don't want them to get dirty, so you buckle a sheep blanket on them. Sometimes they look at you when you're doing that as if to say, "Hey, what's this nutty thing you're putting on me?"

Three weeks before the fair, I start working with my sheep to get them used to walking with me and standing the right way. I try to practice with them every day so that they stand in line with their heads up, their backs straight, and their feet set squarely under them. It makes a difference how you treat your sheep. If you're mean to a ram, he'll get mean. Someday he may butt you! Ewes are more timid. If you're nice to them, they'll trust you and listen to what you say.

When you show your sheep in the ring, you have to keep your eye on the judge because he's telling you where to stand—if you're first in line or second or third. And he keeps moving you around as he judges your sheep for size, weight, what its fleece is like, and how it stands and walks. Once I was sent to the end of the line. Thirteen sheep, and mine was the thirteenth! I just stood there feeling pretty low. You try to make yourself feel better by saying the judge is all off. Judges have different ideas. One judge will pick a winner, and another judge might put that winner in third place. When you win first or second place, you always think the judge is the best.

I showed my first ewe when I was eight. I bent down to straighten her feet, and she took off across the ring with me hanging on. Kurt had to stop her. It was embarrassing. My mom took a picture of the ewe running away with me, and I tore it up.

Right now I'm raising all my sheep for wool. When I sell the wool or win a prize at a show, I usually save the money for college. But if I go to an auction and see a ewe I really want, well, college is pretty far off and the ewe is here, so I buy the ewe.

There's the judge calling for Suffolk yearling ewes. That's me! Here I go.

P.S. I won! Second Reserve Champion. That's second prize. I get some money and the biggest purple-and-gold ribbon I've ever seen. Now my mom can take all the pictures she wants.

A Tip from Todd: *Talk to your sheep in a nice way. They'll learn to trust you, and you can train them better.*

Lindsey and Ardallila

How would you feel if the wish you wished for all of your life suddenly came true? That's what happened to me. I have this friend Glen who's like a grandpop to me. Since I've been real little, I've liked to go to his farm and spend time with his horses. When he bought an Arabian mare by the name of Ardallila, I fell in love with her. There was something about her that was different from all the other horses. When she saw me coming, she'd walk toward me as if she had been waiting. I'd talk to her, and she seemed to like me.

I guess Glen saw how much I cared about Ardallila. One day he said, "Lindsey, I'm going to give you Ardallila because I see how much you love her. But if you don't take care of her properly, I'll have to take her back."

I was so happy I laughed and cried at the same time. Ardallila, my horse!

Glen has a real sweet tooth, so to thank him I baked a German chocolate cake with cherries.

My dad was happy about Ardallila, too. When he was a boy, he

loved horses, but he lived in the city and couldn't have one. Now we live in the country, and he has three—Breezy, Zaabrina, and Ko-Ko. I help him take care of them, so I know what to do for Ardallila. We feed them twice a day with grain, hay, and water. While my dad is away, I do all the feeding.

Every once in a while, we take the old sawdust out of the stalls and put in fresh sawdust. The sawdust gives the horses something soft to rest on, and in winter it keeps them warm. When I give Ardallila clean sawdust, I feel like I'm giving her a clean sheet for her bed.

My dad knows a lot about horses. Breezy, Zaabrina, and Ko-Ko are Arabian mares, too. He told me they're probably the oldest breed of horse. Nomads in Egypt used them four thousand years ago to move across the desert. They would also ride them into battle. Arabians are very strong and can carry riders a long way. My dad explained one of the reasons they're so strong: they have a shorter back than other horses. He said that Egyptian men valued their Arabian horses more than their wives. When it rained, they would take their horses into their tents and leave their wives outside! I guess there weren't many rights for women then.

Another thing I learned from my dad is that horses like to play. You can even buy toys for them in the store. I bought Ardallila a big

ball, and she loves to walk around holding it. Then she'll drop it, kick it, and nudge it around with her nose. My dad's horse, Breezy, likes to pick up pails and carry them around and then drop them over the fence. It's fun to watch Breezy play with our dog, Polly. Polly will grab onto Breezy's tail, and Breezy will shake her off and chase her.

Ardallila is green, and so am I. She hasn't been trained at all, and I've never done any training. I think that's good because we're learning together. I hope to show her in some 4-H shows in the halter class. That means she wears a halter and a lead line, and I walk her and trot her a little so the judge can see how she moves. Then he judges her build. I guess the best way to explain is to say that she's in a beauty contest.

There's a lot to do to get a horse ready for a show, and that's what I'm learning. I brush her coat and her tail and mane and see that there are no tangles. I clean her feet and check for rocks in the hollows of her hooves. Hooves grow like fingernails, and every two months we have to have them trimmed by someone called a farrier. Horses don't need shoes unless they're going to be walking on hard stuff like cement.

To make Ardallila look her very best, we shave her legs to the knees to get rid of messy hair. Then we shave a strip of mane between her ears and a little ways down her neck so that her bridle will lie smoothly in place. Shaving that strip of hair helps show off her long, beautiful neck, too. We trim her guard hairs—those are the hairs around her nose—and even put baby oil on her muzzle and under her big eyes to make them show up better.

Right now I'm taking riding lessons from a trainer, Pammi, who's only fourteen years old. But she knows a lot and is a good teacher. I try to practice an hour every day. It takes a lot of concentration. Someday, when I get good enough, I want to learn to jump. I've made some tapes of jumping shows, and I listen to the riders talking to their horses,

coaxing them on. You can hear the audience shouting and clapping. It's really exciting.

People talk to their horses a lot. I do. I like it when no one else is around, and Ardallila and I have the place to ourselves. Talking to her makes me feel better when I'm in a bad mood. I just tell her what's bothering me, and she looks at me with those sweet brown eyes as if she understands. I can hug her and know she's all mine.

Sometimes I wake up in the morning and think, is it a dream? Is Ardallila really mine? And then I think of Glen giving her to me, and I know it's real.

Glen could have gotten a lot of money if he sold Ardallila. But he says he gets more pleasure out of seeing us together than money would ever give him.

I'm never going to disappoint Glen. And every year on his birthday and Ardallila's birthday, I'm going to bake him a German chocolate cake with cherries. Someday, when I win a jumping show with Ardallila, I hope he'll be in the audience.

A Tip from Lindsey: *Give your horse a toy to play with. She gets bored, too!*

Steve and His Watery Friends

I'm lucky. My grandpa owns a pet store, and ever since I was little I could go there and see the animals anytime I wanted. He has kittens, puppies, birds, rabbits, and a lot of fish. I get to read the books on animals, and sometimes I feed the animals and clean the cages. When my grandpa's busy, he lets me ring up a sale on the cash register.

If I asked you to guess which of all these animals I've gotten the most interested in, I bet you wouldn't say fish. Nobody does. They figure I'd pick out a talking parrot or a puppy. I knew a little about dogs and birds. They were familiar. But I didn't know anything about salt-water fish.

One day when I was at the pet store, my grandpa went to the airport to pick up fish from the Caribbean Sea, Hawaii, and Australia. I watched him put them into tanks. The fish were bright green, orange, yellow, blue—every color you could think of—and different sizes and shapes, too. I knew that I wanted to learn about them, so my dad and mom bought a tank for our house.

With salt-water fish, you need a really big tank. Ours is four feet long, and it holds fifty-five gallons of water. When you set up a tank, you get to make the whole little world your fish are going to live in. You can pick the kind of coral you want in the tank and the color of pebbles or shells. You can decide if you want plants or not. One thing you have to do is make some caves out of rocks. In the ocean, fish can swim where they want and get away from each other, but in a tank they can't go very far. That makes them itchy, and sometimes they attack each other. So you have to give them caves where they can just hang out a while by themselves. It's like when I want to get away from my little sister. I go up to my room and shut the door.

My mom and dad are really interested in salt-water fish, too. My dad's a fireman, and in his off-hours he and my mom set up fishtanks for people. If anyone has a problem, they try to help them. They've taught me how to test the tank water to see if it has the right amount of salt and other chemicals. If the water is missing just one thing, the fish might die. You have to really know what you're doing.

Another thing that will kill fish is feeding them too much. A lot of kids do that. Instead of putting in one pinch of food, you put in two, thinking you're being good to your fish. You're not. When a fish eats, it has to get rid of its wastes, right? And the more it eats, the more waste there is. Waste turns into ammonia and nitrate, and too much ammonia will kill the fish. I've heard my mom tell people who worry that their fish are going to get hungry, "Better hungry than dead!"

It takes a while to build up a salt-water tank. You can't dump in all your favorite fish at the same time. It's safest to add just one new fish a month. I started with a blue damsel. They're fun because you can almost see them growing. One week a tiny damsel, the next week a bigger damsel, and the next week an even-bigger damsel.

When one of your fish dies, you feel awful. You wonder if you goofed up on anything. Maybe you did, and maybe you didn't. There's so much about salt-water fish even the experts don't know. No one knows why the fish won't breed in tanks, but they don't. Maybe it's

because no one's figured out how to make the water in the tank exactly like ocean water. In a way that's all right. I don't know if we should be able to make up nature on our own.

I like triggerfish, but they're carnivorous. I have to know which fish it's safe to put them with. They could swallow an angelfish or a butterfly in a split second. They'll leave the tougher fish like an eel or a lion alone. Something my mom and dad and I learned is that a cleaner wrasse fish will die if it doesn't have another cleaner wrasse in the tank. We figured this out because we'd put a healthy one in the tank and it would die for no reason we could see. If we put in two, though, they'd both be fine. We figured that one cleaner wrasse just gets too lonesome.

My dad is a certified diver, and he's promised that if I keep my grades up in school, he'll teach me how to scuba-dive. He dives in Lake Michigan, but that's fresh water and all you can see there are trout and perch and carp. The place where I'd really like to scuba-dive is the Caribbean Sea. It has some of the most beautiful fish in the world. I'm helping my dad and mom service tanks in the summer and saving my money so I can get there someday. A fireman friend of my dad's owns a diving store, and I like to go there and try on some of the equipment to see how it feels. I don't try on the skin suit because it makes you really hot!

I think about scuba diving a lot. At night, especially, I look at the yellow angelfish and blue and green damsels in our tank and think of diving into the Caribbean Sea with them swimming all around me, as free as I am.

That's my dream.

A Tip from Steve: *If you're only supposed to give your fish two pinches of food, don't give them three or four!*

Neruda and Todi

My name is Neruda, and my rabbit's name is Todi. We live on the second floor of an old house that's been made over to look new. When we moved here, my mom and dad took the small bedroom and gave Todi and me the big one. And it is big! They figured we needed more room than they did, and they were right. House rabbits don't miss going outside if they have enough space inside for running and exploring. Still, it was nice of my mom and dad.

I've had Todi since she was a little bunny. She's seven years old, and I'm ten. I bet I've spent two years of that ten watching her. That's what you do with rabbits. You lie on your bed or on the floor and watch them. I can watch Todi do the same thing, like gobbling a carrot, over and over again and not get bored. I like it when my mom flops on the bed with me, and we Todi-watch together.

Sometimes Todi watches *me*. Rabbits are very curious. Todi always knows when I have a brand new pair of shoes. She walks around my feet and looks at the shoes. Then she sniffs at them. The next thing she does is chew them. Usually the laces go first. Todi can make a new shoe look old really fast!

Rabbits like to chew, but they're not doing it just for fun. They have to chew on hard things to keep their teeth filed down. If they don't, their teeth will grow in crazy directions instead of being lined up right. When that happens, the rabbit won't be able to chew its food and will die.

I don't like to think or talk about it, but that's what happened to the first rabbit we had when I was real little. My mom and dad didn't

know about rabbits' teeth then. Now we always make sure to check Todi's teeth. If they're growing too long, we take her to the vet to have them filed.

Besides my shoes, Todi's favorite thing to chew is a tree branch with the bark still on it. I guess that's what she'd chew on if she were out in the woods. So if you see a branch on my bedroom floor, you'll know why.

Oh, there's something else she likes to chew—my Dad's exercise mat. She found it one night rolled up behind the chair while she was

in the living room with us. We weren't paying any attention to her, and she doesn't like that. She started thumping her foot. It's her way of complaining. We still didn't pay any attention to her, so she started exploring. That's when she found the exercise mat and started chewing a corner off. My dad said she probably liked the rubber in it. I figured the mat must have been like a big piece of bubblegum.

My dad hid the mat on a high shelf, but that didn't stop Todi. She found another piece of "bubblegum"—the pink bathtub mat! She'd climb up one side of the bathtub and slide down the other and start chewing away. So we had to have a new rule in our house. Keep the bathroom door closed!

That's not the end of the story. One boiling hot day, I came home from dance class. All I wanted to do was go swimming, but there was no one to take me. I filled the bathtub with cold water. I had to cool off some way. I was brushing my hair when all of a sudden I heard a great big splash!

There was Todi in the bathtub! She was paddling real fast and holding her head so that her nose stayed above the water. Poor Todi! She had climbed up the tub to get to the bathtub mat, and look what happened. She was one surprised rabbit!

I figured she must be scared because she had never been in more than a half-inch of water in her whole life. I pulled her out. Did you ever hold a wet rabbit? I got as wet as she was. I didn't need a cold bath after that!

She did another surprising thing last night. I forgot to close the cage she sleeps in, and she jumped into my bed. I woke up scared, but then I saw it was Todi. She was using my bed for a playground, running up and down me as if I were a big hill.

Sometimes I wish Todi were a more cuddly rabbit. I would have liked to lie quiet in bed and hold her. She's so warm and soft. But I tell myself, if she were cuddly, she wouldn't be Todi. So I guess I want her to stay just the way she is.

A Tip from Neruda: *Your rabbit needs things that are hard but safe to chew on. Try tree branches.*

Dougie, Isca, and Magic

The kids who live around here are all scared of Isca and Magic. And it's not just kids who are scared of them—grownups are, too. That's because Doberman Pinschers are big and smart and look fierce, and a lot of people train them to be watchdogs. They bark and bark and bark when someone they don't know comes to the gate. When Danielle and I were babies, my mom could put us outside in the yard and Isca would watch us. She wouldn't let anyone she didn't know near us. Mom says she was the best and the cheapest baby sitter.

Sometimes I like having dogs other kids are afraid of. Especially the kids I don't like. It's as if I have special power like those space guys on TV who aren't afraid of anything.

Isca is Magic's mother. Isca had ten puppies, and Magic was one of them. I like to hear my mom tell how they sold all the puppies, but then the lady who bought Magic gave him back. She said she was getting scared of him. I was real little then—four months old. Magic was six weeks old. My mom and dad decided to keep Magic for Danielle and me. Mom says Magic and I got along because we were the smallest things in the house. We grew up together.

Magic's not like Isca. She's not a good watchdog because she won't even bark when she should. My mom calls her a pussycat because she's so sweet and unscary.

Isca and Magic are supposed to sleep in the basement, but they'd rather be in the house. Magic comes into my room and gets into trouble. Especially when she chews the wheels off my trucks. I was glad when she chewed up my church shoes. They squeezed my feet!

Once she chewed up my grandmother's twenty-dollar bill! We buy dog toys for her, but I guess she likes money and shoes better.

The best thing happened. Isca just had puppies again. She had seven, but one died. Isca loves my mom and lets her watch when she's having puppies. That's because she knows my mom is a mother like she is. Sometimes I wish I could watch. But these are the last puppies we're going to let Isca have. She's getting tired of having puppies. She had ten the first time, nine the second time, and seven the third time—twenty-six altogether!

Isca let Danielle and me see the puppies when they were just an
hour old. Their little eyes were still closed. The third day we held them,
but not for too long. Isca watched to see that we didn't take them away.
I like their little tails, but they'll get clipped when the puppies are three
weeks old. Their ears get clipped, too, but that doesn't happen until

they're three months old. If their ears weren't clipped, they'd grow big and floppy.

I don't want the puppies to grow too fast because then I won't see them anymore. My mom is giving one to her boss and one to a friend. And if she doesn't sell the others soon, she's going to give them to the vet so he can find families who will be good to them. Maybe one of the people who gets a puppy will give him back just like the lady gave Magic back. I know which I want it to be, too. It's the littlest one. I don't want to give him a name. I'll get to like him too much, you know what I mean?

A Tip from Dougie: Keep paper money away from your Doberman if you don't want it chewed up.

With thanks to Giselle Hartl, Brian Laegeler, Maya Terrell, Todd and Kurt Schmid, Lindsey Hagerty, Stephen Solberg, Neruda Marsh MacNeil, and Dougie and Danielle Williams for their enthusiastic cooperation as well as to their parents for their unfailing goodwill. Thanks also to Hugh MacNeil, Neruda's father, who came to my rescue with photographs of shy Todi and Neruda.

About the Author

Barbara Garland Polikoff learned most of what she knows about photography from her father who, during the Depression, made his print enlarger out of a gasoline can. A free-lance writer-photographer, she started writing for children when her own three were born. For the past fifteen years, as a volunteer, she has conducted writing workshops in Chicago public schools. Each year, she and the young writers publish *Free Spirits*, a magazine of student prose and poetry. Currently, she is writing a biography of James Madison for young people.

Barbara Garland Polikoff lives in Highland Park, Illinois, close enough to Lake Michigan to walk along its shores year-round with her husband, Alexander, and their Siberian Husky.